Down to Earth

A POETRY BOOK

JOHN WILKINSON

SALT

CAMBRIDGE

PUBLISHED BY SALT PUBLISHING
14a High Street, Fulbourn, Cambridge CB21 5DH United Kingdom

First published Salt Publishing 2008

Printed and bound in the United Kingdom by Biddles Ltd, King's Lynn, Norfolk

Typeset in Swift 9.5 / 13

ISBN 978 1 84771 462 9 hardback
ISBN 978 1 84771 552 7 paperback

Salt Publishing Ltd gratefully acknowledges the financial assistance of Arts Council England

ARTS COUNCIL ENGLAND

1 3 5 7 9 8 6 4 2

Down to Earth

JOHN WILKINSON is Research Professor at the University of Notre Dame where he teaches literature and creative writing, having worked in UK mental health services for three decades. He has been a Fulbright Scholar at the Nathan Kline Institute for Psychiatric Research, and Carl and Lily Pforzheimer Fellow at the National Humanities Center. *The Guardian* described his last book of poetry, *Lake Shore Drive* (Salt 2006), as “multiplex, visionary, ragged, and exceedingly strange because exceedingly true to reality”.

Also by John Wilkinson

POETRY

Lake Shore Drive
Proud Flesh (2nd edition)
Contrivances
Effigies Against the Light

CRITICISM

The Lyric Touch

The light carries darkness
in its pocket

— Ed Dorn

Like Substances

Of its greatness the sun sups of gasoline,
smacking forecourts, licking hearts
lubed with sealed-in blood—break them
methodically, remove while they yet pump,

for each component's certain to outdo
more cautious visions, to exceed or floor
graphs by actuaries: out crawl carers
surreptitiously, welling from their open pit.

Residues flare in asphalt pools, volatiles
spill in parking lots where overheated
agents poke beneath hoods, throw
keys to a collector. They sweat copiously

but let the hearts twitch, pay their dues
then walk, they know how. A flight of birds
ignites against a sunset, blackening
in short order. Of its greatness the sun

asks more to burn, yet more to evaporate:
obedient, oh no wobbling, carers set to,
filling quotas in an immolation park,
smirking by the lines. The sinking fund,

shale library, compress to utmost drops.
Canadian sands crush; heart's pre-emptive
impulses crush too. Thumps consummate,
not a baton's tap. Not the thump at its

life's own pace, no the thumping wakes
votaries to greatness. A snatch, a skip, as
if it rang out true time, as if their crisp
snare were damped, dicrotic but reliable,

sending children forth in bubble-wrap,
alert to metre, calm with methylphenidate.
Organs shall be chained so then output
more effectively. Tuned to work with

willing clouds, willing currents, willing
followers whose mode, touch, hints,
time-keepers constant to their rooted beat,
through transcription move in phalanxes,

delivered by the skip-full only, skips
abundant in this free scrapyard. Just
put everything into the skip, no overheads
trouble offshore derricks when they nod

like a lossless engine in its anaerobic
chamber, turning at a distance, transmutes
nothing into fresh air, field staff report,
overawed. This nothing cranks its shaft,

encrypting data for shell companies,
masking ownership; it comes up in roses,
wafts light & heat with gently-beating
stamina. Should ever timing-chain snag

its unmetaphysical hook, sheer away cogs
shunting children down; sparse gusts of
vapour pegged between stars, will spell
a name suppressed, a child's breath

suspended on the negative, will imprint
the shadow of the cloud morning burnt off.
Tracing invisible writing, sexual spill
slathers grass, gas notates a blind gut,

but a blade shaves earth like cheek or table,
wipes the contract. Could ever air's writ
attract Melaina to the forecourt left
dark for her form, heart she made pound.

Δ

Passerines still fail to break the spiral,
loop the loop. Though yet imaginable as
visitors who thread coloured gases, take
pleasure in the nightfalls, the failing light.

Dogs do also, prancing legs scissor low
vapours, glass has covered them in domes,
torpid rainbows flop alongside winking
gems the beldams of some marsh scatter,

not to leave the dregs unstirred, smog
rolls, suffocating level ground. Down beats
gold on grey panels, down beats the hot
gospel, blessing their demolished kids

garlanded as they festoon bridges, crowd
asphyxiating ducts, a college band's
thump-thump blisters the fleet fingers
trained to carry tunes unto this last; up

the squander surges, candying its light
tulip overflow, then drooling pink & violet
toxins from its lips. The prairies brazen,
stalks stand out like coral, dapple cats

cut across the sun's downtrodden margin,
dodging white patrollers, boys playing
chicken weave trucks, cut down service
alleys, snap fingers at the vigilantes,

sneak behind the corn files, behind rock,
an ocelot impersonator, shape-shifter,
dogs the sun keeps track of, will accept
no flame, or prototype, last or causeway—

wading in alfalfa, plunging through light,
sprint from rock to concrete wall, noiseless
mouths gaping. Gulp oxygen, clutch
water, clutch chocolate. Slinking up on

well shafts. Thumping across loose planks,
feet percussive pound one lap ahead,
future carers harry these who swift to
chug what heat draws, skipping over

pivot-risky slats, stretch their elastic bone,
spring when their oppressor strikes. O
see the motes that mock the swallows,
see the children dressed up to the nines

go forward while the born-lucky scatter
through high grass, kids sweat blood
long before they bow on reddened stone.
Shake you boards! Prophesy, you priests

what was adduced before said, insiders
loop down airy entrails, conscripts of
their past. Light carries, song carries,
carers bear away the stunned in their jaws

to warm Chicago, steam hisses angrily
in blind pipes, knocks through Manhattan,
bled off sates the spectres of futurity.
How will the forerunner react, blanched

in her subservience, drying offerings
racked on poles. She grimaces in lines of
sheets & shirts, a watermark, a telltale
stain, burn-mark of the sacerdotal sun.

Δ

The sun of its greatness would restrict
movement. The sun of its nearsightedness
gets in close & licks the face it pillages
for next course. Proud sun's reserve

army of space-heaters now will field its
Mexicans & Poles, they turn up or dig into
what rainfall or cash-in-hand permit,
lifting tubers in their scant down-time,

who reap some wetted richness by day
turn their hands, turn then to improvise
with shucks of shade against gullies,
tucked inside clefts, hideout near a river.

Behind rubbish bins, fuel distributors
trade their chips of sunlight, gilded
child oblation fuels this energy exchange
in lorry-loads, children at a high point

of blood-standing, all of most, most
reckoned, most admired, irreplaceable,
of soft-pillowed, all most precocious
in astronomy, forever pitched in to scythe—

these gas-holders, fume-breathers, fume-
exhalers sprint round the ball-court
throwing shapes at each other, aching
to feed furnaces, get sent up in smoke:

Corn-reefs half-protect the quiver-nerved
brat who scarpers, neat dodger, gold-
spotted, burnt, dapple-limned ocelot
head-butts a lading gate & fuel tanks,

panting with tongue lolling, edging over
sandy ground, wriggles beneath radar
on his stomach, sand burns & wafts
recompense to heaven; heaven that exacts

life for life, accepts the surplus & spoils,
snorting incense up from furnaces,
the subtilised, the fluted shearing
inwardness of later wreathing substances,

blue gas futurity, stirred up in tornadoes,
cyclones of furious disbursement, kids
tugged off to lymph camps, ripping
down a tidemark's tar & toil, throatily

to sear, drown, clench. Powered by such
zeal, how could they fail to provide,
pressed hard, spun dry, collectors mass
like cotton what children had yielded.

Tide them over. Where blacktop unrolls,
grunt cars. Hear that votive prattle grate.
Car prototypes wink on Mayan floors,
soak up whatever, slopping like a low-

consumption valve, processing the ghost
files, children cupping cheaper gas.
A totem pole resplendent playing out
its bindings of copper. The smirking head

expresses tears. What runs dependably
has its effect, engines flew across parks
from car bombs, scattered shrieks behind;
now newly innocent smiles readjust,

crushed envisaged blessings surge,
sun whose garish splash, yolk calendars,
destroys all hearts, prises open walls
of milk, of blood, oil, rods & concrete.

In Tempo

In this state of exception
arms splay, legs scissor,
all in concert nonetheless.

Beats slip, gears mash,
clutch though they disjoin,
rivulets grip the gravel,
mash conforms to mesh.

Buds will soon regenerate
via his precious blood,
seed the tree they left off.

Strap high clinanthus,
spurious like lost sheep.
Beseech him on this fig
pith I'd magnify forever.

Intervention

How far can any dry pod
carry, how
contemptuous a hand

        deal its green
suitcase trade, bobbing up
to lay & brood,
lunged at on a lark shelf.

Also the holy ghost
acrobat with head-dress
undisturbed,
despite splotched leggings

licked his crown
strobile as the hop fruit.

Present Company Excepted

The leaf agent makes our killing,
well-nourished
mould takes its fill,
& soft snow lowers the bar.

The fish component rakes a neck.
Vouchsafe audible voice.
Our jay-walker
stamps the sky in passing.

Creep underneath like iron lips
dimple earth, ants
vesiculating banks, load
as if sponges, air pods

alongside the toll road,
tangibly a rash or a cocoon
might settle on
fields listing with our casualties.

Stamp of Origin

Ice encroaches, ice tamps,
gear
teeth connect, set in train
the nineteenth day,

sightless birds fetch up on
wild wings,
                    spiral stunned
towards slabs,
                        on mica glints

flammable, inflammable,
the strength of the hills,
shadow fossils
          spiriting away

all passers-by their convoy.

Oversight

The more thought through,
the more a day februate
churns shit. Rocks
drawn tidally, obstruct mouths,

all go to show what's minded to
oversees the spate.
The ram's head quadrant,
hawk smoke day entablature,

traffic needs mouths to stop
subject to remote
nerves: mire bakes hard
beneath the gridlock.

Granite worktops
fritter into blown grit, crops are
shred abstractedly,
heart, not your garments.

Next to Nothing

Lights were scouting the cornices' light
icing because

In East Chicago the dust lids a big take
Yes I'll try poker, try craps

So shape up, scroll into

shape with what you face, a hot-press
fact-clamp rising by each second taller

nose-bone, mouth-bone, ear-bone, drum.

Number One

Blue-gas-embalmed,
that solid blood
jack-hammers seeds,
sinoatrial valve,

bashes down caps
jagged in their casing,
fills a sand sheath.

Fortune
will make smile glass,
faces spread
        composure,

in up to the neck
disarmed,
looking after themself.

Excuse Me

Lined up for the gangmaster at dawn,
set off like a boost of painted pebbles,

faces clatter into runnels, into plough
ridges, burst like sacks of lime

& broken arms & legs, hollow necks
march resurrected. Forces make strides,

swank their nakedness, now the tax-
exempt, I pour my heart out, I do,
boast fruit.

Collaboration

If one more consignment,
hands beat through slats & piercing cries

If one more consignment,
dancing up that long folded ramp like a
cut-throat razor to the capstone

If one more consignment,
larch cramp basket adz ocelot right hand

If one more consignment,
the chinagraph the conscripts' wrist band

I count my toes
I number the hairs on my neck: a minority.

Condensation

These child devourers are not spirits,
but are you & me at heart.

But what holds these men at heart?
just condensations of the spirit,

spirit nothing but the vapour trails
of children, the matter hearts called.

They peck at fresh meat. At mothers.
Then evaporate. Broken & contrite.

The Indiana Toll

Crept from degraded bags, sputtered out of pipes
in soaking bulges spiky roots, warms bolts, frost-
frees the fused plates, ejecting plugs of glacial ice,

aligns them though at odds, ironing out divisions I
for one thought everlasting. Succumb to warmth,
passively disposed because of sun's people, smart

couples, clusters, singletons, affable communities,
each has a lodging place, buys or sells a footprint,
nestled in the shadow of a red rock or green hand.

The layers are sanded sheer, their linen naps tight,
curves take the wheel & the hinterland is promise
past reproof, fortunately no stations, merely stops,

though cats-eyes pop, bridges warp, levees break,
aggressive grilles forge deep welts down four-lane
furrows boiling rivers discharge into, primping up

prairie grass the aimed tornadoes flattened, scythe
mohican cuts, buffalo waves, & gap-tooth railings
crumple: blood-stained rocks, green-bespattered,

lurch & sway alongside, washed from earthworks,
meteors they may be, lumpy vectors splatting life:
is this the best evidence on waking they peel back

their carbon copies to parade? left but the leavings,
labyrinthine trash-pickers find their trash swiped
in trades for new apartments. Mutually dependent

cone sections buried like a dog its bone, prescient
or come to that, produced as if hatched out today,
touched up, licked a little, set in favourable light;

surface never takes the pigment, nor Sue or Katie,
any employee, risks indelible love but so defaced,
which means a comprador must grease his way in

patriotic slogans, teams & bands, the Alleghenies,
heat-bonded overlays machined to shrug pliantly,
to warp in time while owning to but too solid earth,

though smart cones pour out sunlight, furring up
on transcendental poles; presently footage shows
confused drivers age on leaf-fall, overshoot ramps,

these for solos, these for armoured convoys, these
plausibly, were colander for cress, go for saplings
hell-for-leather, since its highs look down on them,

go for stumps ruffed in beefsteak fungus, up from
thoughtful earth the map of undertakings, surface
ghosts whose subterranean bodies fling out spores

since their depths look plausibly like height put on,
how say you blind in scurf, would wrinkled sleeve
puff up like gelatine, a blue January atmosphere

the night's flats distend & fill with stormy flickers,
pavement quilts, blacktop bulges, & its presences
wreathe inky pumice in fine spray or steam wisps.

That was the future, backing deep into a thick sky
as the securely gated, as the reassuringly patrolled
play at corralling steers & heating branding irons.

Δ

Until it stiffed we ran our car heater, burning first
the spare then all the car tires for warmth, Miguel
went for help but had not eaten, so without a hat—

Sue or Kate I doubt. Ramon, José, play their slots,
their slots the chance all take, their slots the altar,
lights ablaze, chrome-crusted, radiant in clearings

spread a make-shift stall, from staging areas post
bites on lunar chafing trays, tuck hors d'oeuvres
in king beds whose perturbations flex; but border

vigilantes drawing on their babies with a flourish,
chalk or lead, blast holes behind an altar triptych,
fucked angelic spirits blip & scuffle truly headless

chickens, o the heck we are, flitting flattened soil
plunge in gullies, crest a foaming ridge, headfirst
dive at straining cars, wriggle into T & pants, tire-

scorch a bottle clearing, grubbing up an underlay
deposited in panic, strike the tents, gather kids,
gun for breakneck cortège. A caravan of fugitives

hotrods its tanks of bio-fuel towards high tunnels
ripening these tulips & tomatoes, the pick of each
graded through the shuttle combs where business

plays out fiercely, bison trains, fenders slamming
obstacles aside, the windshield splatted galaxies
obliterated, buffalo's de luxe trim smashing trees,

now why relinquish such minnow stuff I'd earned
but best invest it in that shadow trust, delivering
returns a thousand-fold from our stake, originals

spread-eagled on the hoods are beasts & children,
ice collects from bloody nostrils, any agent going
sacrificed to bring on roses, distant polypropylene

scoops the productivity from ice-glaze in its plates
propped on edge, across the sky the bees & moths
scrawl the life sentence, cosmic excise hoovers up

dust due. Would its depth-effect enhance on low-
glare panels, feel warmer, much as though insides
palpated, touched through valued sky were gently

slashed with that mare's-tale switch their searches
like a comet's tail drawl? Wheat struts in reap-me
phalanxes, oceans combing down deranged locks

settle into corn-rows, settle in a fish-tank striation,
so lines are laid, but plasma ghosts show through,
insides circulate like burps & farts warm the shed

behind the true solar panel, feed-back sky stapled
perfectly, not one pocket, not one slot, the finest
membrane lets go showers of perspiration in veils:

damp joggers kick into the drift of epithelial cells,
loop skid-marks, etch blinding furrows with their
burning glasses, superficial drapes, prototypes of

more fields, electronic prairies, page paging page.
There will be work. There will be school. Rammed
along its folds, the bedroll underpins the landscape.

∆

Stay diligent, & once you start digging don't stop,
once you aspire, a magellanic cloud spatter spits
geometric figures. Intensities they hurtle through

distort the air & bend them to inflections of their
traces, orisons in triplicate drape about the mole
of the port of entry. Coning paper in my fool's cap

shielding from bombardment, each splash creates
a phenotype its transferees peel off, so I copy you,
this has to be a block the snow obscures, wrap up

warmly, scatter round the quadrats then examine
meteorites like sunk, inverted heads, carbon bolts,
graph the plumes of steam, y-intercept, a slope's

lapsed loveliness. Test points will now draw pluck,
draw their line at a solution region, they partition
woodland with a gut garter drawn to snap, screen

for larger particles, those with built-in switch-off
squandered in a sky-writing, fail, as if the output
digitised in touch-buttons, click-wheels, overtook

catches in the throat: chew before your suspicion
takes the biscuit, take whatever life throws at you
like Mother Courage, risk-controlled bits anyway,

swallow them at once, quick! now I perform a flip
that like a pastry-cutter, *minus infinity* that edge,
its cadence shaped by air's concerted loss, carves

away the otherwise congested, cones below whose
apex kids left behind were factored in, registered
impartially: what cute additions! we admit the lot!

consume the nebulae the spotters crush or thickly
daubed in sunstroke. Viridescent trash, squat red
numbers block our way like bollards. Coated skies

reek of sour laundry, wired & serviced hinterland
shocks fleeing rodents, blurt skin embosses roads,
pigs tricked out in head-dresses bash into vitrines,

laden breezes long & perfumed heave their series
of regressions, not your verticals! not your slants!
who'd want to know about what depths you rise to,

drying over canvas. Stretchy skins. Stern mothers
convolute the open plains, meat-packing mothers
help each other get by, María doubles for Dolores

who feels sick, spatulating gloop on baking sheets,
absorbent pads where giblets slap in shiver cities,
now tear off your pink copy, Immigration Service

kept the top, & freedom more pressure-sensitive
by moments, whirrs within a packing plant, a biro
scribbles on the parquet as unmarked cars creep,

rut down the snowy street between frozen sidings,
scrutinise the temporary vinyl & polythene glass:
freedom gathers at the hard edge, grates against it.

Wipe, wipe, wipe. Snow quilts a quadrilateral, icy
needles infiltrate so-weary flesh. Wipe, wipe, wipe
the clouds re-scanned digitally, a rock-solid image.

Δ

I hold still to course though twisted in fear's clutch,
rictus grip on whose face unwarped by mnemic air,
I hit a deer & hurtled off the road into a soft ditch

re-formed me pink & quickly like a dentist's mould,
cops pulled me over, soon the further shunt impact
brought them to their senses but their senses went

out the window, like you find you landed up before
the date due, you reaped OK, you understand the
portent, a swagman pivots posing on his back foot

spraying rocks with his urine, *camine, no camine*,
this hall he bangs together, market values were his
caper too, take off him that mucous rock hammer,

chip at blacktop, cloisonné, a gilded crust, its core
of mimsy pink & white, fistfuls of others' coupons
plunked on the desk will forge a passable identity,

I had not thought so many for one person. The one
stands up in weary sheaves, signs along the dotted,
staggers for his cool cave or climbs a sacred mount,

finds this town beneath the aegis of black Artemis—
bees are heard, the rosemary spikes out, crocuses
stud seasonless green fields: then if he dare stray

flickers will secure him, her dithyrambic lightning
gloms onto her subject, buzzing at the frequency
her previous victims set. The stamp paper monkey

pulled out of his tailspin, leapt towards his *1st mark:*
steely, tight of mouth, he was so highly-sprung in
twisted shroud, he ran dauntless to retrieve, a dog,

a total dog to summon, *2nd:* musing over obsequies,
brushing wayside epitaphs & bunched blossoms;
so we screw our twists of airy loss, the heat-waves

scribbling us against the wall, its candy courses will
confine us to their pattern, *3rd:* how say you, lost
mouths tricked out with almost-say, once adopted

fell off in a sheaf of coupons: no sweat, no elbow-
grease, no front, no cartoon. That's the shape of it,
his papers make him legal & unseize that windlass

shelved above his bed, hung from the upper world:
press the nipple to release the fibres dragging out
upon his mind like substances. Familiar cold start

coughs & wheezes, turns, first lowers its filaments
into his juice at breakfast, piercing manky sheets,
melts the plastic visor hooked above a bricked-in

loading bay, then bears down on the defenceless
indiscriminately. Some go unquestioned, wraiths
of our memory, this one a sister, & my step-father

was that hind I hit. Within their seats, passengers
got visas in my name—I'll fly like paper, get high
outside their frosted windows. Chrome flaking off,

now my skin flakes too, that means concupiscence
bears hope, bears repeating. I flit behind banners.
Share-croppers file North along the Natchez Trace.

Back of Beyond

Birds need to place their calls,
& when connected,
download different ring-tones
in shared space, yammering descend,

    lickspittles,
    quarter-hour
    repeaters,
    pilferers

trespass incommiscible within range,
whirr round the chatter
streaming through junction boxes,
in & out to take calls.

Laughing falcon. Ivory-billed
wood creeper.

Travel Plaza

Lipped or canted space
soon forsaken, shamed, oft reviled,
warps about the sticks
like a delinquent bear
on the Toll Road, struts & rolls,

        star sprinkle:
        uniform:
        psoriatic
        scales fell

It's for the birds to sort out.
The Pototoc was for the birds only,
this field, the trees are for the birds

squalling over fat pickings.
Thick-billed seed finch.
Pistis Sophia drives a Hummer.

Stopover

Hard up against it
        saliva stirs
air bubbles
crush against the palate
streaming by
the pillowed ear—

Hard up against it
        busses pass, the
smell of fingers
brushing nostrils,
        itch on the
foot sole

Hard up against it
        face the marble
abstract,
the polished share,
        feldspar

Anechoic.
Pee-wit. Pee-wit.

Rust Belt

All 365 heavens

packed the biggest box
then whipped, herded off, yes
gone into ellipsis
        hem with a blowtorch.
What's left now lumbers,
hugs outer parts,
patch compliance, patch
through the demiurge

a rigid designator
emptied of its blood's sound
        volatile as spirits,
charged with traffic
& then crushed:
he sees himself as self-father.
Still can breath reform

from breakers' yard as
substance cast
over light that shines
        without shadow
through your love, Diotima?

All Those Gates

Despite the target setters
crouching in their
trenches, serving time

invisible accumulators,
overloading, spark—
the one is named assembly.

It all went above my head,
custodian of blanks,
the more rising break

points to an unadopted
unincorporated tract,
ever before my sight—

        poke-tongue
dreaming in its real estate.

The Confronter

Where seed capsules float,
                    hoick air's
doubtfulness, go scattershot
like warm air lifted larks,

We spill out, we trespassers
                    we loiter
hooded oriole, blown off-course

skank shank the fender bender
softly depressing asphalt,
others jig foot to foot
in bright summer flummery,
        a windhover flakes too—

Fretted bass, a conga rap,
kicking off the rondo
calls resistlessly,
        echolocates us
        across stumble fields.

Crumple Zone

All markers struck away
by rivers' rising,
stakes shear & bright withies
twist about

Whither for the roach-
mounted rubies, fob-dangled
cameos, the crust

gold had larded, wriggle,
stinging their retainers,
pins out of stocks:

Affluence broke anchor.
Flopped pedals,
passion bottles,
gilt lapel badge, the brush—

flagged shrubs all afloat
flit into the dusk.

Like by David Smith

Every day I retreat to 420 Sunset Drive. What spirits,
what woman, what fruitful interest ravening, what
class formation, what country, ragged self that clacks
provisional wings while supervening from yet higher,
bilks me out of pampering my rug, my breakfast bar,
my gas range built into the patio wall, & listlessly I
pat the dog, uncork a bottle, seldom glancing at the
place of origin, varietal, the date, it's hard to satisfy
the massage chair, the home spa dribbles dilatorily,
a kidney fuels a television, flutes that were my eyes
scratch the mirrored surfaces while foul water pipes
back up disappointed, what suppressed my first flush,
the lost wax fell away & I was hard, gleaming, crying:
Why not eat, rubbish stirs below foot, its skirmishes
& fallings-out betray its need to find home, freshets
locked & scrimped, drain exposing their undergirded
stolid organs, tamper-proof the seal will reinforce
an obdurate myth of purity, the loom fires & shunts,
tweaks micro-magnets into line. A garage door lifts,
I fine-tune the sprinklers, my Peruvian maid spirits
up today's mail. This must be 3264 Country Knolls,
the mail is right, it's I was misdelivered, misbegotten,
spirits pinched my passway or the sky woman sang
from her rock above the dustbowl & a home sauna,
O Amelia it was just a false alarm. We feel depressed,
a chalk bluff shrugs its run-off down voided streets,
a waste-compaction site, grassed over, lost to local
memory, scalloped into putting greens, contaminates
play-areas in safe squares. Disposable diapers swell,
soar in green & silver twists, but no appurtenances
put down roots, neither linen press nor chiseler's bag
nor tumble-dryer raises vent or hose, nor will shape
the satisfying pile, if clouds are Rodinesque the rocks

look puffy & the bridge has misplaced its confidence
slap into this limbo, but I'd put my shirt on invisibles,
package up hot air then pass off risk, put an inside on
the hedge we pitch towards, for we'd abjure opacity,
blurting fat, air, fire & words, from satiety to vacancy
surging & retreating through the fireflies & crickets,
scanning for M'Shell Ndegeocello, Lorraine Ellison,
my ears, my heart, my stomach, senses want dialysis.
I had been coated in encaustic, recently egg-smeared,
I download, I up-sample, trip through neural switch,
in every dream home its Philip Guston pail of blood
stews rancid in a chill-box with its vestige of warmth,
a phosphorescent rot devours the fumes & leakages,
it looks like green, it looks like the primeval prairie!
I quench the green shade, intruder lights must check
a lakefront garrison of red rock, enforce a lock-down:
O I shall flush my liver, melt to bullion, steel myself,
I shall fill the slopes with a barbaric herd in raw steel.
Remotely the flicker of an eyelid switches on a light.
Remotely be careful what you wish for, not because
you might get, because the needful might converge
in still-ticking hearts, each with its jellyfish mantilla
sweeps in a red tide from the west, desecrating shore
or eyeballing it, visibly engulfs the limit of the visible.
I can watch, convict, care, preempt, levitate in metal,
undercutting hilltops shadowing the clock. Trestles
fold up treacherously, armchairs shift edgily beneath,
their feet are not planted, their views are blindsided,
a cocksure but recumbent form scoffs up an officer
who blagged his way, the chair he sat in became him,
thumbnails of those tortured morphed to mug-shots
of torturers, it is not the tiny hill I think the world of
nor the temperate clime that birthed me I renounce,

but my supports, what kept my crate aloft, I'm flying
off my handle, take amiss, planes create the structure
scaled to lift misfiring hearts, grass & air & plentiful
spring water: fabrications lift off from Studebaker's
silent yards in stainless steel, place of birth, ethnicity,
my very name, my face, refracts in joints & elbows
difficult to track these days, the wells brook no face,
such crooked turns, such marquetry a swoop revives
abundantly in warm dusk, from mall to river cohort,
indigenous to what, a native dance, uninfected slope,
guiltless town, things were complicated, O things are,
& more so, & I'm weary of such watch. Great rivets
punch the patchwork planes, see! geometric farms,
here come the planes, Amelia! women's songs spark
velocity. Why every day I retreat to 420 Sunset Drive.

Harlem Air Shaft

How choppy! Treacherous! Needles of uncharted
water had lain siege, flossing gaps. Winds purse
mouths for one moment, then a jumbo portion
breaks mouth, their circle grins away, paper floats
                    play & bob
up round the slot slackens, slot fixing to discharge
compellingly its chicken cargo, plucked & burnt,
awaits a more productive fault, juddering to crease
an inlet mapped out like Exploit me! Parchment
                    marl
settles down a ridge & thins, the one furnace feeds
four turbines squat upon the banks, they infuse
veins snaking through a catacomb, veins the Tiber
flushes, organs underneath the godly, multiplied
                    blueprints.
How deluded! how debased! how piteous! Spirit,
white spirit, oil chimeric shimmers & its peel-off
backing prettifies what's dredged up. A mortgage
floats over the pile of trash, taints & lies, cadmium
                    decocted
through laughing rills. I strip away the film guard,
I leave my car, directions I drop blithely in a bin,
babies kick upon heath & marsh, yapping hounds
drag them through the gorse into this lair, tightly-
                    bundled
honeybees secrete wax, & wasps chew over paper,
only ink is lacking before land fills with the record
of the land, water darkens, all accounts are frozen,
warmth beats back to ventricles, twists of sherbet,
                    nitro-

glicerin, a flitched bill of lading queues onboard,
is this whole invoice complete? Sprigs of rosemary
& clove-studded orange to the nose, masters don't
look up, they study figures. You have your papers,
all in order,
to the registry you lead the shackled you imported
off the mappa mundi edge, the Apennine is flag-
draped, are these bills of sale or are these mighty
deeds, their blazon flops like palms or else flutters—
tickertape
which wraiths of slutty viruses & proteins sharpen,
populate through iris recognition. Surface feeders
shimmer over sealed lips, now it's their wannabee
wants shrimp on top, bellows through felted doors,
22
belowstairs! strapped to the bench & hemp-cuffed,
take the oysters, take the porterhouse, a modicum
or less. Flee the meat extraction pumps. Saintly
exudates. Spirit lie deep but clotted, lie impressive,
dwell in
pouches, pipistrelle or cave-born, mud in your eye,
know your tenancy relies on papers long rescinded,
bleached or crumbling where the clandestine bats
sound out their home territory, a dry grotto theirs,
lost lease,
clatter of fall forest, whooshings from the mouth of
a pythoness, her souls ascend to patinate the roof:
How terrifying! How they suffocate! Defenders
of the north sector's slots blow out their hot breath,
my own wings

suffocate us, food chokes, plackets of small change
accumulate, weigh on thought like anchored lead,
press on our minds like substances, so by analogy,
Thames mud, bats' flutter or a chirping mead, rills
                    pleating, bunch
like temple courtesans who putting it about, swing
lead should it be flipped or if a kid had bought it,
years of lead, ramped into a stadium, a bathhouse,
long tresses trailing an infectious, traumatic comet
                    scapegrace
venting clotted cream & steak, stuffed into a cone
sags, retaining no outline. Load on the periphery
still in chains, spirit sicklies over. Springs cough,
the wounds are knit. Made of bandaging a swaddle,
                    out of
an imprimatur's red deck scuffing knees, beeswax
covered me so what I roll in fabricates a roof I hear
humming in the document, testifies to long song
drawn down an inner sea, my black Mediterranean
                    blots & scumbles
laps against
        overwritten shore
a pestilent buzz
        errors in transcription construed as hope.

Like Feeling

Yours to kiss. Yours to breathe. Asbestos
fibres, spiky thistledown, flock amidst
the alveoli, hang out breath in gasps
tethered to the lean-tos. Too constricted,

far too lightweight, hold their breath
amidst the drifting temporising leaves,
puckering & wrinkled. Sleepy kids shake
open on the thermals, international drafts

ripple fields of lucerne. It is a new climate
dawns, envisage its world acolytes,
prowl on outcrops tight in snowy vests,
igniting tips of flame that bait intense

arclights, trained along the pebble ridge.
Enjoy! Trample freely! Sun's convulsions
splurge their incandescent surplus,
seas will carry forth on burning rafts

flotsam of a downturn; sandbars warp
as waves crash over fathers who almost
spent, must now hold their breath &
rub foolish lamps, who gouged of savings,

set adrift by coastguards, bedevilled by
imperious camións & brutal coyotes
break against shingle. Some bank on
acquaintance with land's edge that strikes

then run aground, paving driveways
Mercs crunch, their pebble-dash faces
misted over, trodden on, snatching
at each gust of air, puff & drag, heave hard—

might patinate, might corrode, might scrap,
stretch out to nuzzle that mild light
shoals gird against them; mudbanks shift
to scuttle rafts, ill winds are marauding,

hurricanes named Milagros, Dolores,
rake water, gas blowback blocks the lungs'
honeycomb, on ice runnels cars skid
ending at a sea wall's gap-tooth final ditch.

Unheard wind skitters down a chalk cliff's
bronchioles. Gossamer weighs heavily
on here-&-now, the bell precedes the hour,
a bell's bell follows. Flares & flash fix

the breath-takers, mummified in sunlight
flesh shrinks to thin legs of hypothermic
children, teeter down their climbing
frames, haul themselves on merrygorounds

clutching wraps of brown powder, eying
with salt-crusted eyes that afterstroke
timed to bring them back. In wicker
baskets, hobbled birds squawk, the sterile

seed gets scattered as though seasons yet
work their patch, yours to sow, yours
to reap between stones. Smoke wreathes,
flops across swimming pools, mopping up

reflected light, obscuring shadows past
the ring-road: under towers of silence
splay gasping children, stand they must if
dawn breaks, against its callous projects.

Δ

Glass deforms beneath its own weight,
worms of light burrowing a travelled optic,
seek to converge. Are they ghost travesties
infest the far-distant procreative body?

Things go blank, a burning tar underlay
was suddenly suspended. The roads merge
bedazzled, choked to this crawl all seek
to reproduce remotely, faltered men

shower at their stopover, female hands
pull scant comfort. Truckers flock towards
a lead-lined hot container, heedless of the
moon strapped wonkily against a rig—

a flight of moons, frozen in their circuit,
shaping shade within whose scoops &
niches, wrigglings proliferate. Each man
hymns his moon for the white offer'd milk,

baffles of shamefacedness swing aloft
their gauzy veil, worms rut a monitor
by time-lapse. This portable high-power
floodlight helps direct. Cars we see collide,

will they concoct new bodies, genuine parts
as though designedly? The piecemeal
lumps, reproduction crashes inward,
to adjust uses accident: a freak or floater

put through modification so oblique,
has time to band together, flourish, plunge
back on itself. Turn about: its other cheek
will follow, sun melts the tarry tundra;

but at dawn the indefatigable women milk,
hoe the little plots, fold down silver
soil before the temples, stint on water
for their children. A shaved moon swings

above the cabs, a bulk moon will supervise
workers pushing on through daybreak,
smooth your dimity skirt, struggle into
overalls before Phoebus strides & burns

carving up the six-lane highway, one choice/
impersonate or fade, one choice/ vapour:
Now shape the notes. Swing your burden,
lift your chorus, part the mouth to take

its strain without words. The moon tos-&-
fros, the flapping shutter breathes. A heavy
moon yaws over men at second jobs
hanging out in pool-halls, garage doors,

backs of theatres, nightclubs, dragging
on hot drinks, subbed till whenever,
uncollaring a six-pack, discussing last night:
the ever-present moon still alters shape,

still touches revellers who claim to sing
obscure script, transcribed faultily off
floaters nailed against the day, their version
baffles sun & light rigs: but can it remedy

the fane of Tescalipoca, that was erected
with human skulls, cemented with blood,
the highways too, the railway tunnels
lined with cartilage, no moon compensates.

Δ

Whose beauty is deposited on drenched
lawns by solar edict, daubed over roofs
between the aerials & dishes, sluiced
yellow leukocytes on walls? Some defer to

the beauty of outputs, while indirection
casts a more gentle spell. The source
primeval lavishes the balm it scarfs up,
bestows gouts of insatiable consumption.

Clouds venture forth as silver rocks
float across a trading-floor. No beyond
advanced from the distant circle, only
boulders bob like buoys at the perimeter:

self-consuming can't restore that rift
by putting out. From rubble burying a car
they will stagger, toting glass vessels
drooped from the eye to tease the press,

& where the moon shifts, ganders off,
spills burn into car hoods, & under seats
propane cylinders with heat jackets
wait for the phone to chirp, children

dance before the call connects, the sonne
schedules its fix of unalterable truth
scoring welts over armadillo backs
prostrate in work & in worship. Daily

rituals of the canyon, ledged adolescents,
lubricate the dry spring. Much-favoured
lips pout before their idols, packet
fire glams their every orifice as moist,

& a prepared offspring will be their surety
prospected in the blocks. Hypocrisy
bonds the prayerful with hedonists,
shifting goods like down a sushi track,

smashing through rubble for its wafer lode
of credit, goods in heaven, goods on tick
flap through rafters of the trading floor
drawing fire, then will doves descend

in a goblin market, show their hearts
to day workers; claiming kind for kind
they pluck out stones, for this is rapturous
energy transfer at work. Airlanes conduct

to LA, barrios will air-condition Texas,
try-outs glamourous as Mixcoatl
leave their ball court for the antechamber,
shaping up for sacrifice with sun's chop.

I hear them call from every skip, I hear
them when I skip a beat, the beat is theirs,
the thump against the basket, the basket
calcifying, arteries are hardening like

coral, hear them moan in compaction
machines, hear the hiss from valves
in the soil of the brownfield site; & in skips
charged with rubble, intervals of throat

clutch, the intervals of palate strop, the
full skips of the disregarded, scarcely
noticed, lunar run-off shines like mercury.
Balloons float in a shrine in Pittsburgh.

Δ

Yours to cough, yours to feel the brunt,
inch down the column, spitting cobwebs.
Where are you luring me if not into
your home? My tongue cricks on the obol.

The proteus will hear its way, the olm
called human fish, flicker in the fractures
between sheared strata. Spawning blind
to starlight ricochets down chimneys.

Within the denser scars, the calcified
bracts breathe. Words! a light-pen is too
compromised, tactile feedback, click,
scufflings in the cave. Then at the console

cave bacteria mix the phosphorescent mat
warm to shelter migrants pressed by
whitened walls. Bats don't venture for
rich pickings, proceeds are for the birds

strictly: ostentation is the style they follow
in birds' echelons, what's sweltering
from shanties, fizzes over Las Vegas
lawns, channelled across condo lobbies,

raised against, set against trading loss,
asset-stripped, siphoned off & processed
offshore, piping through invisibles,
sweats beside this very fence this evening,

their persecuted proceeds. Daring reivers
dodge through no-man's-land. An ocelot
disdaining border law, stuffs his cheeks,
then slips across like boys with rifles

race for cover once cloud evaporates,
shake tourists down, *cementeros*, scurry
back to rubbish heaps, these proceeds
fenced off from the ominous suburbs, fuck

stridently in open view, have no bed to
crawl into, the owl hoots, the twilight
tumbles through light's yawning jaw, dawn
recurs with its terrible systems of belief,

whose proceeds kill in all good faith, feed
the feathered serpent: kids sacrifice
themselves to lure back the sun tomorrow,
crossing dumps, the cack metal dumps.

As palely fades the moon, sun draws up
to light a way towards the terminal: a drab
monocle sinks, motorcades peel off
then steam in garages: the choiceless

forced to choose, choose scorched earth,
prostrating at full stretch to greatness,
raised then stricken down. Insatiably
the sun feasts on these equatorial caskets.

Bats flit & tongues beat, yours to capture,
yours to sing the confused & the future;
deep lines were drawn, blasts shook
damascene low rills, rebuffs from brass

blazed upon the bass; a collective susurrus,
you get in full blast from an airshaft, one
huge loudspeaker, gasped out voices
bleeding, sapping, redeploying North.

Ravenous At Noon

The warm flanks of trashed cars,
                                                  the hot leather,
blue leather blistering like bee stings proliferate.

I wait in liberty, the straddler of a garbage dump,
pitted like with silver fillings,

intricately wire the graven boss, but it works free,
flying to the tailgate party.
                                          Were these my fillings,
no offense,
                    broken out of rank ascend to feed
cementeros, glue devotees, pitterpatter down
on idling defaced backform heads,
                                                    slick raptors?

Or cased against the day, the crescent
drained their attributes & spirits of the graveyard,
rows of nipples risen on her chest like bee stings.

This my rival.

Hunter At Dusk

Melaina, down your paths of fire the children shuffle,
senses nipped in the bud—

hard as nails, while in the sky walk the women
bearing skulls blood-filled. The sky glows red.

O how free I am amidst the yapping dogs.
Broom pods crackle. Rivulets of molten glass solidify.

As it were a fresh brake.

Lying In Late

Tree leaves ripple, combed through by unfelt breeze.
Artemis, it must be.
Surely got a nice smile, but loopy dirty
                                                  played a blinder

by my reckoning, she cuts & shuffles & some
bastard cuts me up
          trampled
just before the ramp. My face drains. My usual front
sent down the plug in sexual spasms.
Nowadays a deprecated feature, as it turns out.
Seems that deity wants payback & with no ifs or buts.

Drifting Out

They whet their knives. They scrape past. Just as I did.
They sing but denounce in passing.
        They contend like water.
Quiet down.
Down the air shaft, bright pink the cap
keeps covenant as does a furnace.
                                        That's the seal I press,
the red webs form its caulk.
        Scored surfaces capitulate & furrows
soon submit.
A powered hub, what waits for me is straw,
                a book defrayed,
custom retreads, hands shaping hieroglyphs
for a tip-off: I see a veiled woman peer
from her attic window,
flutter glances down the lawn,
cast off her cheek when bitten, throw it in the balance.
I came from nowhere. I did not want a gap but a niche.
No powder, no polish, but to be collected.

I lie below the relay station, Goonhilly Down.

I stand on white steps.

Duke Ellington strikes up Harlem Air Shaft in Fargo.

The hillside hums, the rotary mowers go back & forth.

The Defeat of Artemis

In moneyed college towns, to orient holds sway,
organs lumped as sculpture, fleer at their origins,

open still to scrutiny in lit lines of the inside-out
persuaded to make much of utilities & input jacks,

scrub first person plural withering back to stalks.
I am assured. The day revolves as if a natural fact

self-monitored, caresses round each cherishable
like a car wraps a tree, trees surround burst cars

in clearings formed for art. Trees strain out noise
from a field hospital, damped with cheery daubs

where tightwad creeps within his cartoon, scraps
with bigfoot for an eyeful suspended off a gibbet,

fingers itch after umbilical trade, his hob-nailed
liver studded callously with pigeon's blood gems

fetched its price, kidneys travel for their homes—
here 'home' denotes returns from trash combers

cannibalised, which means made something of:
so a mounted exhibit gains aura from that dump

children pick over outside Nablus or in Tijuana,
a sponsoring foundation made its pile there too.

Blight powders each, coating softly, aluminium
paint shines in feathery tags on weathered steel,

or where a neon tube slants purple by a crossroad,
turn that way to reach the meat cabin, one kidney

will be speeded in its ice box or surge more loftily
through formaldehyde, but from what track's side,

from what dump, from what child's pouch, scrolls
the lengthy gloss subvening on a snort of appetite

unabashed, the long term perspective, partnering
necessity, democracy, from now on pull in organs

from afar, final assignees can't be identified—nor
can donors giving lives, who also stay anonymous.

I have a place outside Santa Fe, I ski in Colorado,
for the most part I keep an eye on my investments,

bronze face, brass buttons, gold teeth, the gashes
gleam ruddy in the Congo, in the Amazon. Floppy

fins stand up on modelled flanks, light lards a trim
hood, crisis starts with patient lay-out of elements

we need, the beating heart of derivatives degrades
materially, the stretched pelt flaunts its resistance

in taking off, I saw those systems crash & burn as
suited jockeys, suited geeks ran for the maproom,

ketamine tornado, highly localised, groove a path
through grey matter, or for dread of being chilled,

left alone by trappers, by the lumber middlemen,
the cast-out wolf children howled round the camp,

emptied of hearts carved flambé from the breasts
to the groaning board, prowl white internal casts

of packing for their ripped contents. A loom rusts
vivid in its glade, king snake slithers through each

valve & slit, see how the structure holds because
eyes dart & dart, a watcher figures out its position

as if now summoned. I plunge my face in hot coals
while in the sun's eye our syntax shuffles forward,

assuring the day's revolution. Back away, you cry,
re-erect the totem, but the unconditional reaches

after the traysful of embers then bestows them on
the living cowled in the definite light, nominative.

Δ

Great is Artemis. Her temple will be lead-shielded,
purlieus sealed in UN safekeeping, permanently.

Seal the hot springs & ice over the distinctive rills.
Their spoilage will compress into bars & blocks,

smooth tablets marked with component time-code,
heat must be contained, leaching of excess water

spun off from expressways & steeply-raked fields.
What's buried never rots. The dead cavort on film,

prancing down the beach before the consistorial
elders, they'll milk them like they're plump aphids,

they'll drink anything to stay active, laugh at death
when jilted again by heartthrobs as the reel turns:

Great is Artemis. She feeds us our compensation,
spilling silverly in furrows. But her temple is shot,

clad within its concrete Parnassus. Games persist,
the velvet stage trots out Lipizzaner miniatures

& toy poodles. One more encore shouldn't harm.
Return these to the video vault, tick box for Billie

Holliday, request the Leontyne Price, take out the
grandparents, take out Emmett Till, temperature-

assured to never die, subsist in chains of zeroes
countermanding the deep chain of one, Artemis:

ritualistic stoning, nooses drop, clouds disperse
cold triggers over peach groves, breadbaskets etc..

Great is Artemis. Her life is squander, her people
work their butts hard to rankle her riddled flumes.

Her most militant snorkelled off Phuket. Bar-girls
turn tricks before chamber mouths & love-bomb,

servants of the bitch of Ephasus. Great is Artemis.
She takes fierce bends on mountains on her 650,

she holes up deep below the finances, disburses
through the vents & cubby-holes, risks life & limb

to prostitute herself, she has spread herself across
the *temenos*, across the piste, she extracts what-

ever lucre these moneymen might still lay on her,
gobbling the jackpot, sliding, ribboning the Alps.

Great is Artemis. Springtide dribbles through the
egg flint embankments, rills along their ditches.

Bond issue oozes out of silos, pours into valleys
waste disposal companies strew with wide limbs

she loves to see root-confused, it's her advantage
played by gulls & traders swooping at the plough,

cattle egrets blown off-course, wrappers chucked
from roundabouts, buckets-full of chicken wings

comply before the off. Accumulation's demigods
stand dignified while strafed on blaring podiums.

Lenses bulge. Many of them bogus, went direct
from id to item, still their fear conforms the lanes,

fear of the non-recording angel, violent vacancy,
so all stuff themselves, no crack or gap or mouth,

that's great. Then we thaw. For great is Artemis
who never watches, never looks in wing-mirrors.

They are the road's curves that steer my car. Tatty
triangles of grass alongside interchanges, serve

notice, serve her through a dot matrix, rampant
rusty prophetesses stretch arms studded red with

nourishment or pain's swellings, lumps flare up,
fizzle big with heat. Milk them. Great is Artemis.

Δ

The goddess slumps. Her day also comes to grief.
On hot granite & on solar panels children watch,

crawling out of moss the gas valves poke through,
searching their own images beside a pool urgently

shaking off its oil slick, grading the new windfall.
Banks of cloud gained the most from hurt feeling

eased into their database, fine-tuned the shade of a
cast of thought, drew the tongues from openings

clacking out identities; still beneath the watershed
freedoms evaporate, the panacea sprays like spit,

threads lead only into webs, organ caul that wraps
dry sand. Athwart their deferential heads, a torch

reducing me to silence, shed doubtful light before
a miserable stick, scrapping dogs, a swag of bees

draping Lenin's bust cockeyed in a park of kitsch,
buzzing in unison with buzzing entranced pylons.

An updraft whirls excited voices from a basement.
Crust & rind sing. If downstairs had been caulked

with cement, growth erupts in surface pockmarks.
Glass & chrome sing. Behind the scrim I heard air

voicing, air was sibilant. A chewed coinage sung.
Surface models are constructed on rescued bones,

their hushing sap bolsters layer on layer, it turned
out their maws of rubber fuse, their webbed fingers

lunge for cocks, rummage in a tenantless breast,
poke at loose moss like second thoughts on prime

metal, how such things corrupt from inside! Lingo
costive, blabs their mouths but silently, the captive

tongue utters shoots, yellow aconite splits trodden
faces laid as flagstones for a statue of Anonymous,

crumbling cement. So what rises as with one voice
from cast-iron gratings, from the hold a saxophone

hoarsely honks & shudders, now I know grit that
stings my eyes & won't allay, sinters into hot slate.

A man was stricken down before Anonymous. I
heard a branch break, heard the swarm dispersing

dash its outline upon slate. I up-ended the stones,
filled a blank slate with clash of metal eye-blades,

mental process, my bushy optic fibres flash. Ichor
supercharged, sends its cars out to curb my reach,

where's the wake, why do the mutes drag their feet,
each gapes, no smacker, no embrace, this parody

shows the sigils of authority on its hat-bands, webs
all in fat. He quit the service station, sniff, he had

himself updated, spread his sensory ruff, one mite
larger conscious scope. Did he gain in substance,

amplify the signal? Was he a credit, made for joy?
Brakes hiss, trailers shunt, reversing beep, truck

tectonics grind & puff out hot air baled for export,
no-one caps the wellspring's throat. Hail its riser,

crown its distributor. Slinky closed loop field shut.
Air makes these sweat within mountain chambers,

fossils glow like elements. Wetbacks & airheads,
rubber burners, burnside hackers, spa aficionados

feast on the generational gift, such knots of energy
pack the igneous floor, the geothermal halls surge:

This is the house we've worked on every moment
we can spare, sphagnum shoes our converging feet.

Δ

They dodge, great Pan himself, Artemis & Made
Mouse, what kept them, what damped their steps:

their telltale tread goes muffled, they dissimulate
for us though visible in stag-horn skitter, audible

at roadside niches in long rain & shadows. Shouts
to order raise heads from tinkering, command us

leave non-user-serviceable innards, deaf & dumb
we plod impervious to the chirping native songs;

I also grubbed through dribs & drabs, for shucks
of standing interest, jabbered into vocative grilles,

fiddled bones, measured beaks, packing off to lab
specimen spoor. The coastline is construing tides,

the pantheon gapes hollowly within coral groves,
I should edge a prow through mist towards a statue

in its temple, spray re-blinds her in involving veils —
all the crank machinery of blood & gas exchange

hoodwinks me as I approach, I make my presence
felt with sound, magnetic roses amplifying bursts:

what have these herms to say to surface-dwellers,
fearing for our hearts, that they might stutter short

at the power of a thought of depth. Their engines
had been heat-sealed, the surface helped distract,

measured soon as seen, hammered so a weak spot
would vibrate—mute it, damp it, fade it, that decay

in its dying foley walk, pins back the fruit-bearing
boughs & trusses spurs, would any blossom, spike

gesticulate from walls, orbs of intensity convolve
from a particular step, from his loved awkwardness

re-echoing down a bramble path, whose standstill,
radiantly expansive, glistens with telluric charge;

his quip, his laugh, his song, shape the long ellipse
like a soap bubble stays. Glints of murmur caught,

meals snowballed, things she'd often say, Fat Boy
he smiles, I was never fat, I'll eat two cackleberries

(eggs), that was just how he spoke. Similar quirks
broke his stride, so raucous calls from a hedgerow

break through dazzling shifts, their idiosyncrasies
sphere each as with corporal flame. Sparrows hop

on the pate of Anonymous, onlookers run forward
        helping a man who buckles,

(Fee Dawson's voice interrupts,

honorary convict at Sing Sing
        teaching men in shut-down
to listen through their silent roar,
                                cordoning off the engines.

        I'm dazed when the orchard stirs

beneath moss, dappling cheeks, the lips,
        or patinates a sow's
row of teats,
the chiselled piglets
        squirm in light off
chipped, bellied limewood, squealing . . .) If what's

substantial dies the death, what's like substance is
a different matter wholly, born of mien not means,

like substance manifests itself, sow-like, bird-like,
heart stung into its full breast—Great is Artemis:

as if the like were the hawser that transmits strain,
as if the like were a dark sheath, as if the claustral

furnace vents its plumes, in as much of an orchard
as still whispers, from earth's decaying underfoot.

Bound South

In light, in darkness, quarried equipment
        makes a stand
etched in light, etched in darkness,
        cooling after manufacture
then usage. Warmth became conciliatory,
        not soon enough,
for previously the forced air's
        change of setting
cracked, crazed, dragged filigree damage.
        In keeping, sharp curtains
ridge impassive, similarly clothing
        holds its creases, crumples,
looking for all the world like that world's
        definite hatching, dry point:
the under-surface heat churns
        behind plaster, bedposts
worm-riddled, rims of fashionable fittings
        bubbling rust. As always
the ingenious world settles,
        settles for its scurriers—
it's feasible to reconstruct as if conditions
        stayed constant,
glassy spheres like castors turned,
        zero loss through friction,
the slick interface prevails by fits & starts.
        In fact the whole economy
needs sharpened senses,
        so I lie encased & restless,
hatched in mind whose pressed demands
        for electricity, tax for roads,
cries rising off the flat table,
        headers stacked funereal
into the in-box, charges, these reductions

pinch & shape—janitors of
skin-held intelligence, tattoo artists,
Demiurge's sidekicks
scurry home into their nooks. So sensibly
the scurriers settle down
to score sleep, to float their cover stories
with a controlled spin
spheres waltz along to,
just so long as a blabber lap-
top won't be discovered in the public bar,
the harmless freeway potholes
bulge & pock while SatNav rides
the camber, O its dream cadences—
anyone drives in his sleep!
but this guy jolts under his covers,
this jackass driver
scatters, shatters, flocks of goats
tussle by stone-blocked
artesian wells for the merest trickle:
I might be strapped in surgery
or strut like Giacometti manikins in ranks,
grim figures like my shaving self
get serviced by hot
glass, chalcedony or diamond, brilliantly
accentuate, pitch up
in a marble fountain's depths: excellently
bright, perfectly pitched:

Great Artemis, you whose improved worst
skips, blots, makes errors:
Great Artemis, the pre-select who
ceaselessly restructures
matter's elements, whose nuclei, electrons

compose by your fault.
Great Artemis. Pressure now
accrues for change of state,
heat increases concrete-capped within the
chain perimeter, the memories
of bedposts, chintzy linen
forcing thought back into line,
that murky self-regard secures the human
mask, establishes its silhouette,
the animal snarls & wastes
interstitially. Great is Artemis.
For turning in her purlieus & thrashing on
her bed, this procrustean
logic organises, here
distressed the monad stretches
& shudders, basalt stacks slot beneath the
flibbertigibbet sun.
Falling in their pattern, waves race,
the day yawns, sunny despotism
staggers in on itself.

South Unbound

What lies ahead blanks out,
        doesn't make it blank or total washout:
in our car, dented drink containers,
        clamshell box, kleenex,
        scrunched-up directions, are we
here yet, grandparents
        fumble nappies, naked babe
sprawls on a comforter, can you pass
        the wipes. Yes we're here,
we pick up where we left, saying 'we'
        like this or that, we
love blackened grouper, we adore
        biscuit & molasses,
sat-on food-guide shedding leaves, we nod
        off so often, jolted
back to wakefulness as high beams
        saturate our sweat-mapped shirts
momentarily. This face I want to see
        fresh. The gradient
of longing gives me pause,
        the clinch roll hesitates
before the noisiest of mouths (mine
        qualifies), still, the car
reinforces outside with its gecko tread,
in swinging to this outlet,
holding to this ramp, interpolates
        sky's ozone pitch,
hanging off streaked clouds,
        yes I see behind glass,
        behind gracious streets tumble
kids tangled up, seductive
        & unwashed. But on the porch
happiness,

we find ourselves accommodated.
Factory sirens toot across the delta.

Training a heartless killer's easy,
        training killers with a conscience
gets rough. The same applies
        to doctors or whoever. The air crew's
faces break, Slav & slave names
        gleam on vinyl folders & crisp shirts,
but their faces break,
conceiving incidental damage, hands
        shake spring-loaded keys,
& if I agonise with
toothpaste, turning on a tap,
        flourishing my check-list
of threatened fish,
        Mud Slides Block Access,
End of Year Donation for Clean Water—
        So could it be collateral
aid trickles from my clothes rack,
        my shoes start a line of shoes
in Bangladesh, every credit card use
feeds a mouth: no risk one like me
        might slide a hatch, or
raise a platform in the silo. Most
        ease themselves with thoughtfulness,
me included. As a whole.
On the whole.
        On top of things.
"We have unknown collaborators."

What stretches
        forward rain baulks, with greater fury
lashes glass, obliterates

sight of the road: What slides,
what flickers over side-windows, travels
        like a small town in harness
or in step—
not scenery but more a side-effect—
I don't remember driving over railway tracks,
even so beside
clapboard weathers well enough—
        I didn't drive
        through no pearly gates,
cement of spirit slaps up a church
        alongside, elders' coffee club meets,
then like the fall whirls past in russets.
What strikes me
        shut into the car's inside
narcolepsy
                what strikes
dégringolade
                de-
compensation
                long words:
merging left shrinks shadows into porch steps,
curlicues of trapped music
        kerb-crawling through my sleep.
Whatsup.

Grizzled types watch the car pass, sigh
for out-of-state freewheelers,
        sigh for their curtailed children
yet feel justified,
& as the sun spills thirstily on blacktop in front,
        the car barrels onward
as if it were a lamp of earthly flame.

Acknowledgements

Summoned by the writing of this poetry, two remarkable books came to hand: *Mississippi* by Anthony Walton and *Across the Wire* by Luis Urrea. Also valuable were the exhibition *Caras Vemos, Corazones No Sabemos / Faces Seen, Hearts Unknown: The Human Landscape of Mexican Migration* at the Snite Museum of Art, University of Notre Dame, 2006, and a bootleg video of William Kentridge in action. David Lloyd pointed me towards Duke Ellington's *Harlem Air Shaft*.

No table of contents is provided because this is a singular work. But there are titles, so as to have it both ways.

I am very grateful for a Carl and Lily Pforzheimer Fellowship at The National Humanities Center, 2007–8, and for the contributions of my colleagues there, witting and unwitting. Including Maudie, much more than colleague, much more than kind.

CHAPEL HILL, NC, MARCH 2008

www.ingramcontent.com/pod-product-compliance
Lightning Source LLC
LaVergne TN
LVHW041345080426
835512LV00006B/620
* 9 7 8 1 8 4 4 7 1 5 5 2 7 *